OSPREYS

BY CONNOR STRATTON

WWW.APEXEDITIONS.COM

Copyright © 2022 by Apex Editions, Mendota Heights, MN 55120. All rights reserved. No part of this book may be reproduced or utilized in any form or by any means without written permission from the publisher.

Apex is distributed by North Star Editions:
sales@northstareditions.com | 888-417-0195

Produced for Apex by Red Line Editorial.

Photographs ©: Shutterstock Images, cover (bird), 1 (bird), 4–5, 6–7, 8–9, 9, 10–11, 12–13, 15, 24–25, 26–27, 29; Unsplash, cover (background), 1 (background); iStockphoto, 14, 16–17, 18, 19, 20–21, 22–23

Library of Congress Control Number: 2021915669

ISBN
978-1-63738-146-5 (hardcover)
978-1-63738-182-3 (paperback)
978-1-63738-253-0 (ebook pdf)
978-1-63738-218-9 (hosted ebook)

Printed in the United States of America
Mankato, MN
012022

NOTE TO PARENTS AND EDUCATORS
Apex books are designed to build literacy skills in striving readers. Exciting, high-interest content attracts and holds readers' attention. The text is carefully leveled to allow students to achieve success quickly. Additional features, such as bolded glossary words for difficult terms, help build comprehension.

TABLE OF CONTENTS

CHAPTER 1
ON THE HUNT 5

CHAPTER 2
LIFE IN THE WILD 11

CHAPTER 3
CATCHING PREY 17

CHAPTER 4
TAKING FLIGHT 23

Comprehension Questions • 28

Glossary • 30

To Learn More • 31

About the Author • 31

Index • 32

CHAPTER 1

ON THE HUNT

An osprey flies above a river. It spots a fish below. The osprey dives down toward it.

An osprey's wings can stretch up to 6 feet (2 m) wide.

The bird plunges into the water. Its wet feet grab the fish. The fish is slippery. But the osprey holds on tight.

An osprey's feet have pads with sharp barbs. The barbs help grip fish.

When hunting, an osprey may plunge its whole body underwater.

An osprey's wings can make an M shape as the bird flies.

The bird lifts its **prey** from the water. It carries the fish as it flies. The fish will make a good meal.

OSPREYS VS. EAGLES

People sometimes confuse ospreys and bald eagles. The birds look similar. Both have white heads. But ospreys have dark stripes along their eyes. And their wings bend during flight.

Like eagles, ospreys have hooked beaks and yellow eyes.

CHAPTER 2

LIFE IN THE WILD

Ospreys live across much of the world. They tend to be found near water. They might live by lakes, rivers, or coasts.

Some ospreys live near fresh water. Others live near salt water.

Some ospreys live in cities. People often find their nests on telephone poles.

Some ospreys travel more than 4,000 miles (6,400 km) each year.

Many ospreys **breed** in northern areas. Then they **migrate** south during winter. But some ospreys live in warm areas all year.

To breed, ospreys make nests. Females lay eggs in the nests. They guard the eggs. Male ospreys hunt. Then both parents hunt after the eggs hatch.

Ospreys build nests in trees, on the ground, or along cliffs.

Young ospreys become adults after six to eight weeks.

KEEPING THE NEST

An osprey might lay eggs in the same nest it hatched in. Its children may use this nest, too. Each time, ospreys add sticks. The nests can become huge.

CHAPTER 3

CATCHING PREY

Unlike most other birds of prey, ospreys eat almost only fish. But they eat a huge variety of fish. Some fish weigh almost as much as they do.

Ospreys usually eat fish that are between 4 and 12 inches (10–30 cm) long.

Unlike other large birds, ospreys can flap their wings to hover in place for several seconds.

Ospreys hunt in **shallow** waters. They **hover** 30 to 100 feet (9–30 m) above the surface. Then they dive.

BAD SHARERS

Osprey eggs hatch at different times. As a result, one osprey is older than its siblings. It does not share food well. Younger osprey can **starve** to death if there's not enough food.

Ospreys typically raise two to four babies at a time.

Ospreys catch fish with their feet. They use their sharp, curved **talons**.

An osprey's outer toe can rotate. It turns backward to help the other toes grip fish.

Ospreys dive feet first. They stretch out their long legs.

CHAPTER 4

TAKING FLIGHT

Ospreys fly back to land to eat. But taking flight from water is hard. And fish can be heavy. An osprey's long wings help.

Ospreys often fly up into trees to eat their prey.

To fly up out of the water, birds must use lots of force.

Most birds flap their wings up and down. An osprey's wings can rotate. They can flap side-to-side. This helps the bird fly up from the water.

BENDING WINGS

An osprey's wings have a **joint** in the middle. It moves like a person's wrist. It lets the wings bend and turn as they flap.

Eagles sometimes fight ospreys for prey. Eagles take fish from ospreys in midair.

The feathers on an osprey's wings have stripes of color called bars.

Ospreys also have oily feathers. Oil and water don't mix. So, ospreys can quickly shake off water. With less weight, they can fly away easier.

COMPREHENSION QUESTIONS

Write your answers on a separate piece of paper.

1. Write a sentence describing how ospreys hunt their prey.

2. Would you want to see an osprey in real life? Why or why not?

3. What do ospreys mainly eat?

> **A.** eggs
> **B.** fish
> **C.** eagles

4. Why would it be hard for birds to fly up from the water after catching fish?

> **A.** The water is much lighter than the air is.
> **B.** The water is harder to see than the air is.
> **C.** The water and prey can weigh birds down.

5. What does **slippery** mean in this book?

*Its wet feet grab the fish. The fish is **slippery**. But the osprey holds on tight.*

    A. hard to hold as a result of being wet
    B. easy to hold as a result of being dry
    C. hard to see as a result of being small

6. What does **confuse** mean in this book?

*People sometimes **confuse** ospreys and bald eagles. The birds look similar.*

    A. to see an animal in nature
    B. to think one animal is another
    C. to change an animal's shape

Answer key on page 32.

GLOSSARY

barbs
Sharp, pointed things.

breed
To come together to have babies.

hover
To stay flying in the air in one spot.

joint
A part of the body that connects two bones and allows for movement.

migrate
To move from one part of the world to another.

prey
An animal that is hunted and eaten by another animal.

rotate
To turn around or move in a circle.

shallow
Not deep.

starve
To become ill or die from not enough food.

talons
Long, sharp claws that birds use to hunt.

TO LEARN MORE

BOOKS

Huddleston, Emma. *How Birds Fly*. Minneapolis: Abdo Publishing, 2021.

Patent, Dorothy Hinshaw. *The Call of the Osprey*. New York: Houghton Mifflin Harcourt, 2020.

Sommer, Nathan. *Eagles*. Minneapolis: Bellwether Media, 2019.

ONLINE RESOURCES

Visit **www.apexeditions.com** to find links and resources related to this title.

ABOUT THE AUTHOR

Connor Stratton writes and edits nonfiction children's books. He loves observing birds wherever he goes.

INDEX

C
coasts, 11

D
diving, 5, 18

E
eagles, 9, 26
eggs, 14–15, 19

F
feathers, 27
fish, 5–6, 8, 17, 20–21, 23, 26

L
lakes, 11

M
migrating, 13

N
nests, 12, 14–15

P
prey, 8, 26

R
rivers, 5, 11

S
stripes, 9

T
talons, 20
toes, 21

W
water, 6, 8, 11, 18, 23, 25, 27
wings, 9, 23, 25

Answer Key:
1. Answers will vary; **2.** Answers will vary; **3.** B; **4.** C; **5.** A; **6.** B